EASY GUITAR
WITH NOTES & TAB

TOP HITS OF 2019

13 HOT SINGLES

ISBN 978-1-5400-6459-2

HAL•LEONARD®

Visit Hal Leonard Online at
www.halleonard.com

Contact us:
Hal Leonard
7777 West Bluemound Road
Milwaukee, WI 53213
Email: info@halleonard.com

In Europe, contact:
Hal Leonard Europe Limited
42 Wigmore Street
Marylebone, London, W1U 2RN
Email: info@halleonardeurope.com

In Australia, contact:
Hal Leonard Australia Pty. Ltd.
4 Lentara Court
Cheltenham, Victoria, 3192 Australia
Email: info@halleonard.com.au

STRUM AND PICK PATTERNS

This chart contains the suggested strum and pick patterns that are referred to by number at the beginning of each song in this book. The symbols ⊓ and ∨ in the strum patterns refer to down and up strokes, respectively. The letters in the pick patterns indicate which right-hand fingers play which strings.

p = thumb
i = index finger
m = middle finger
a = ring finger

For example; Pick Pattern 2
is played: thumb - index - middle - ring

Strum Patterns   ## Pick Patterns

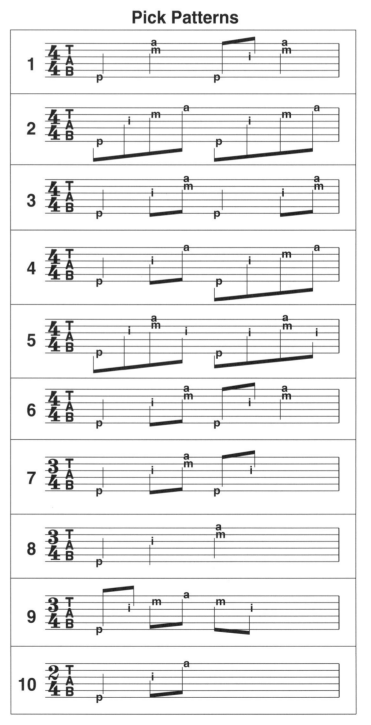

You can use the 3/4 Strum and Pick Patterns in songs written in compound meter (6/8, 9/8, 12/8, etc.).
For example, you can accompany a song in 6/8 by playing the 3/4 pattern twice in each measure.
The 4/4 Strum and Pick Patterns can be used for songs written in cut time (¢) by doubling the note time values in the patterns. Each pattern would therefore last two measures in cut time.

CONTENTS

Bad Guy

Words and Music by Billie Eilish O'Connell and Finneas O'Connell

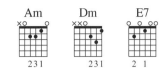

*Tune down 1 step:
(low to high) D-G-C-F-A-D

Strum Pattern: 5
Pick Pattern: 1

Intro
Moderately fast

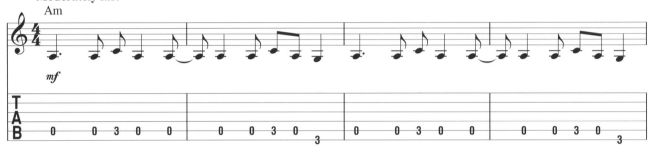

*Optional: To match recording, tune down 1 step.

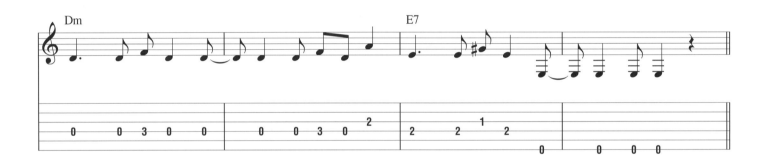

Verse

1. White shirt now red: ___ my blood - y nose. Sleep - ing. You're on ___ your tip - py toes,
2., 3., 4. *See additional lyrics*

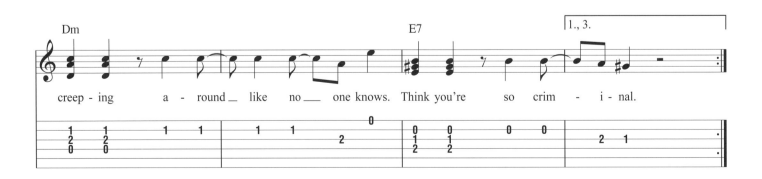

creep - ing a - round ___ like no ___ one knows. Think you're so crim - i - nal.

1., 3.

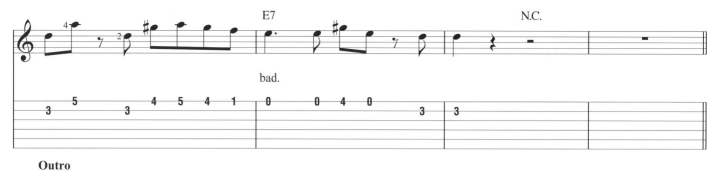

E7   N.C.

bad.

Outro
Half-time feel

Spoken: I like when you get mad.   *I guess I'm pret-ty glad*

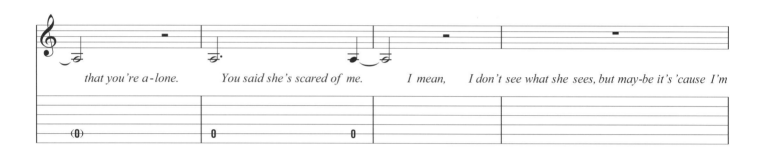

that you're a-lone.   *You said she's scared of me.*   *I mean,*   *I don't see what she sees, but may-be it's 'cause I'm*

wear-ing your co-logne.   *I'm the bad guy.*

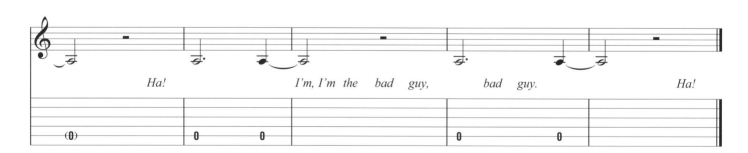

Ha!   *I'm, I'm the bad guy,*   *bad guy.*   *Ha!*

Additional Lyrics

2. Bruises on both my knees for you.
   Don't say thank you or please.
   I do what I want, when I'm wanting to.
   My soul, so cynical.

3. I like it when you take control.
   Even if you know that you don't own me,
   I'll let you play the role:
   I'll be your animal.

4. My mommy likes to sing along with me,
   But she won't sing this song.
   If she reads all the lyrics,
   She'll pity the men I know.

I Don't Care

Words and Music by Ed Sheeran, Justin Bieber, Fred Gibson, Jason Boyd, Max Martin and Shellback

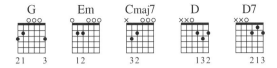

*Tune down 1/2 step:
(low to high) E♭-A♭-D♭-G♭-B♭-E♭

Strum Pattern: 6
Pick Pattern: 2, 5

*Optional: to match recording, tune down 1/2 step.

1. I'm at a par-ty I don't wan-na be at, and I don't ev-er wear a suit and tie,

yeah.   Won-der-ing if I can sneak out the back.   No-bod-y's e-ven look-ing me in my

eyes.   And you take my hand,   fin - ish my drink,   say, "Shall   we   dance?" Hell,

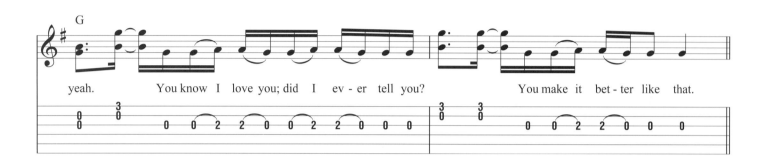

yeah.   You know I love you; did I   ev - er tell you?   You make it bet - ter like that.

𝄋 **Pre-Chorus**

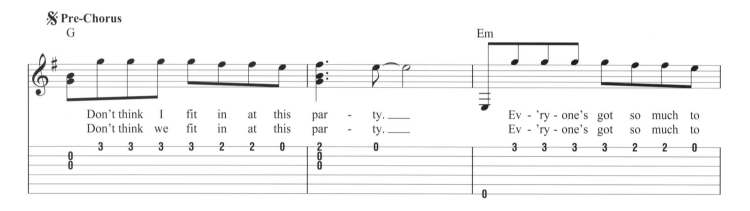

Don't think I   fit   in   at   this   par - ty. ___   Ev - 'ry - one's got   so   much to
Don't think we   fit   in   at   this   par - ty. ___   Ev - 'ry - one's got   so   much to

say,   yeah.   I   al - ways feel   like   I'm   no - bod - y, ___   mm. ___
say,   oh, yeah.   When we walked in,   I   said, "I'm   sor - ry,"   mm. ___

Chorus

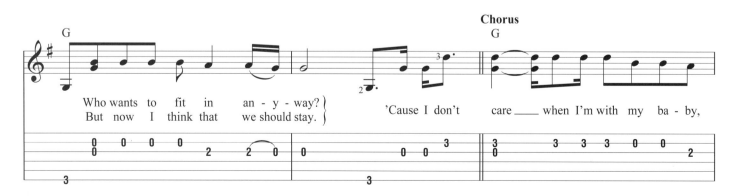

Who   wants   to   fit   in   an - y - way?   'Cause I don't   care ___   when I'm with my ba - by,
But   now   I   think that   we should stay.

8

yeah. ___ All the bad things dis - ap - pear.   And you're mak-ing me feel like   may-be I   am some-bod - y.

I can deal   with the bad   nights. _____ when I'm with   my   ba - by,   yeah. ___ Oo, oo, oo,   oo,   oo,

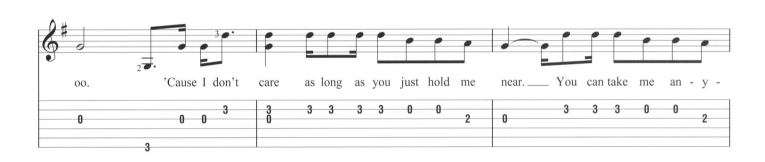

oo.   'Cause I don't   care   as long   as you just hold   me   near. ___ You   can take me   an - y -

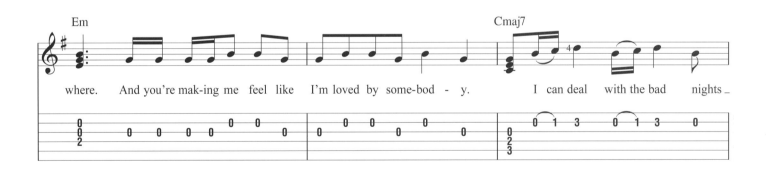

where.   And you're mak-ing me feel like   I'm loved by some-bod - y.   I can deal   with the bad   nights ___

To Coda ⊕

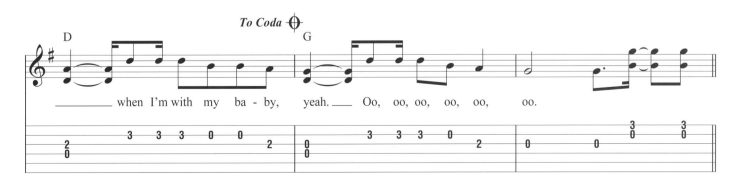

_____ when I'm with   my   ba - by,   yeah. ___ Oo, oo, oo, oo, oo,   oo.

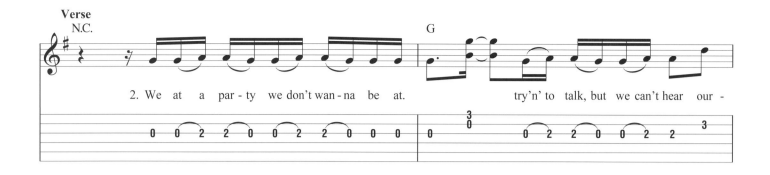

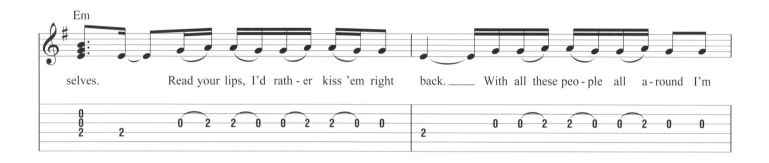

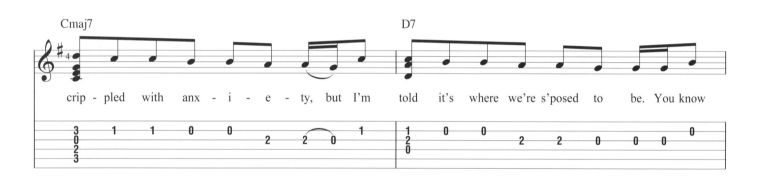

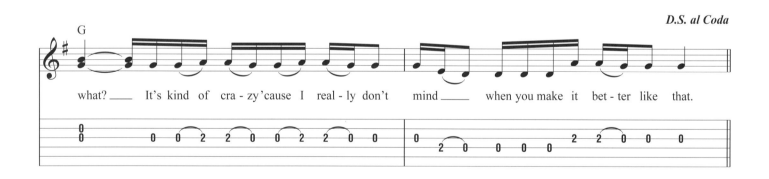

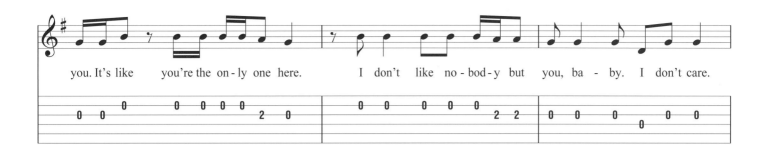

you. It's like   you're the on - ly one here.   I don't   like   no - bod - y but   you, ba - by.   I don't care.

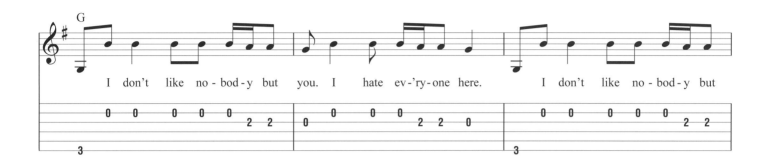

I don't   like   no - bod - y but   you.   I   hate   ev - 'ry - one here.   I don't   like   no - bod - y but

Outro

you, ba - by, yeah. 'Cause I don't   care ___ when I'm with my   ba - by,   yeah. ___ All   the bad things dis - ap -
care   as long as you just hold me   near. ___ You can take me   an - y -

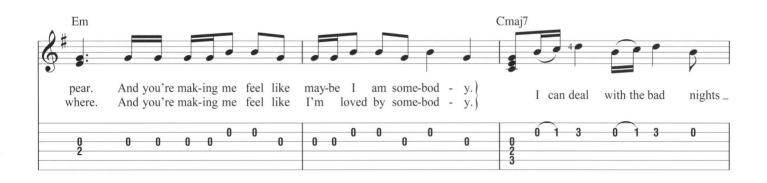

pear.   And you're mak - ing me feel like   may - be I   am some - bod - y.}
where.   And you're mak - ing me feel like   I'm   loved by some - bod - y.}

I can deal   with the bad   nights ___

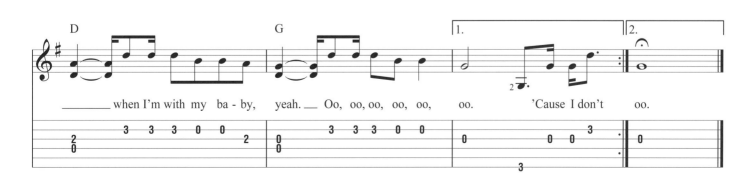

___   when I'm with my   ba - by,   yeah. ___ Oo, oo, oo, oo, oo,   oo.   'Cause I don't   oo.

Beer Never Broke My Heart

Words and Music by Luke Combs, Jonathan Singleton and Randy Montana

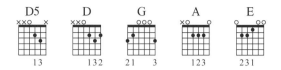

*Tune down 1/2 step:
(low to high) E♭-A♭-D♭-G♭-B♭-E♭

Strum Pattern: 3
Pick Pattern: 3

Intro
Moderately slow

*Optional: To match recording, tune down 1/2 step.

Verse

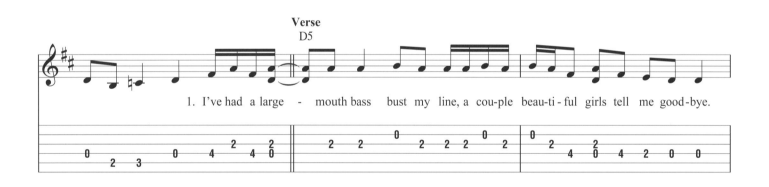

1. I've had a large - mouth bass bust my line, a cou-ple beau-ti-ful girls tell me good-bye.

Pre-Chorus

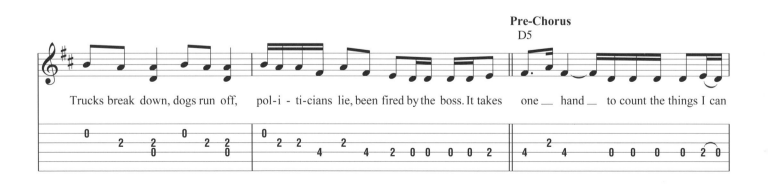

Trucks break down, dogs run off, pol-i - ti-cians lie, been fired by the boss. It takes one __ hand __ to count the things I can

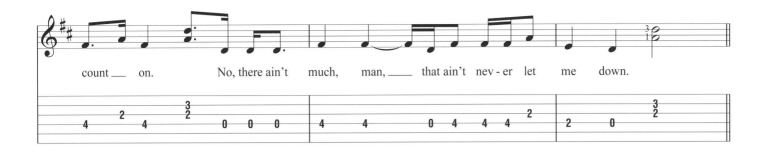

count on. No, there ain't much, man, that ain't nev-er let me down.

Chorus

Long-neck, ice-cold beer nev-er broke my heart like dia-mond rings and foot-ball teams have

torn this boy a-part. Like a ne-on dream, it just dawned on me that bars and this gui-tar and

long-neck, ice-cold beer nev-er broke my heart. 2. She was a Car-

Verse

- o-li-na blue-jean ba-by, fire in her eyes that drove me cra - zy. It was red tail-lights when she left town. If I

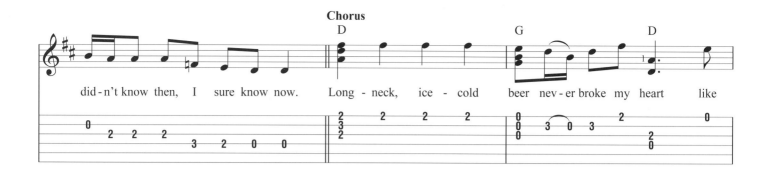

didn't know then, I sure know now. Long-neck, ice-cold beer never broke my heart like

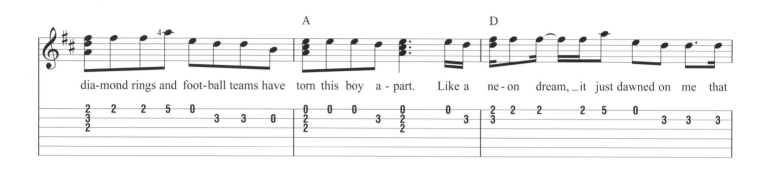

diamond rings and football teams have torn this boy apart. Like a neon dream, it just dawned on me that

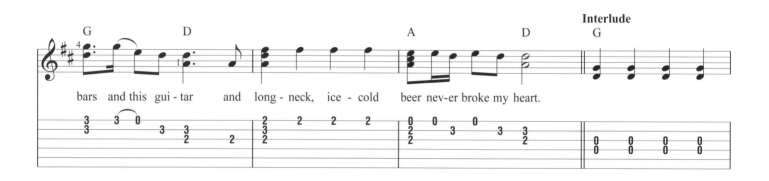

bars and this guitar and long-neck, ice-cold beer never broke my heart.

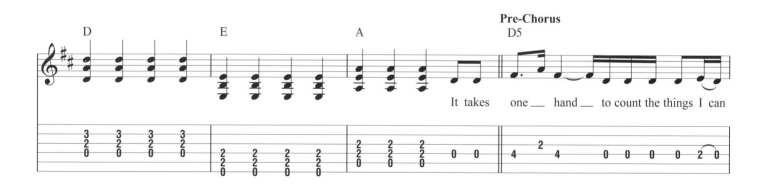

It takes one hand to count the things I can

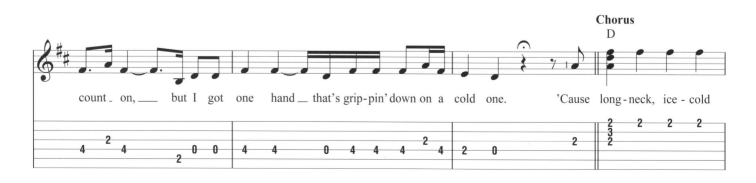

count on, but I got one hand that's grippin' down on a cold one. 'Cause long-neck, ice-cold

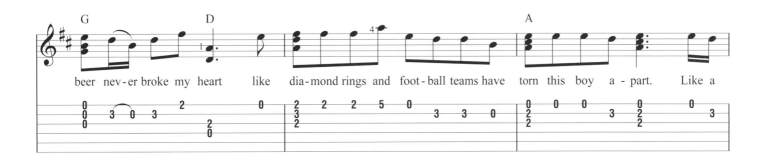

beer nev-er broke my heart like dia-mond rings and foot-ball teams have torn this boy a-part. Like a

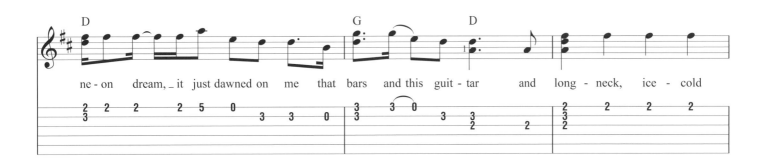

ne-on dream,_ it just dawned on me that bars and this guit-tar and long-neck, ice-cold

Outro

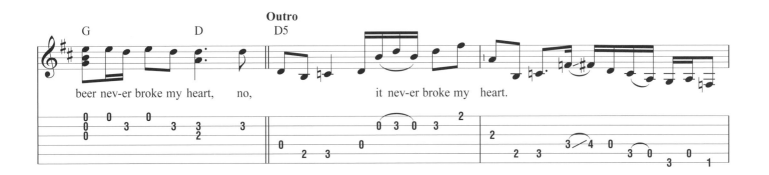

beer nev-er broke my heart, no, it nev-er broke my heart.

Gloria

Words and Music by Jeremy Fraites and Wesley Schultz

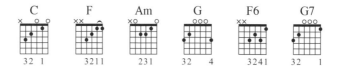

*Tune down 1/2 step:
(low to high) E♭-A♭-D♭-G♭-B♭-E♭

Strum Pattern: 5, 6
Pick Pattern: 4

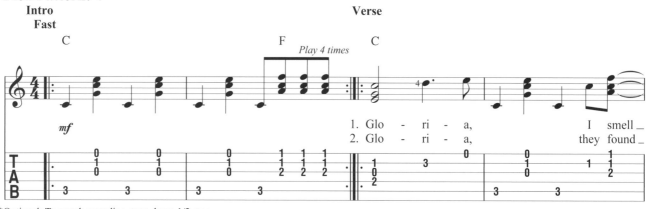

*Optional: To match recording, tune down 1/2 step.

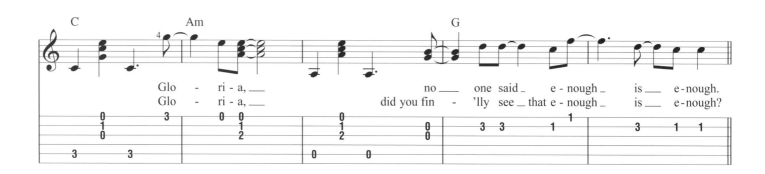

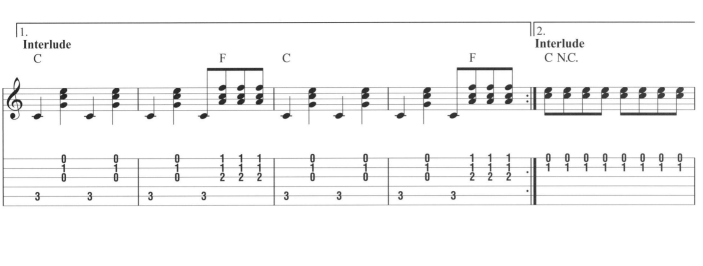

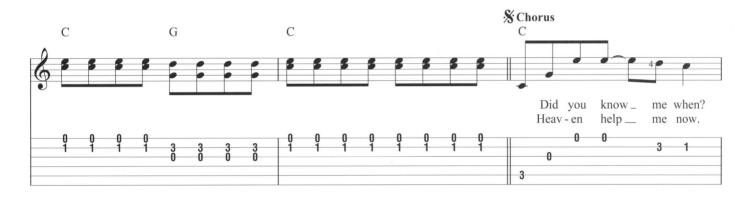

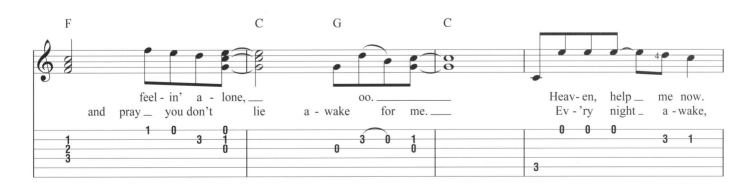

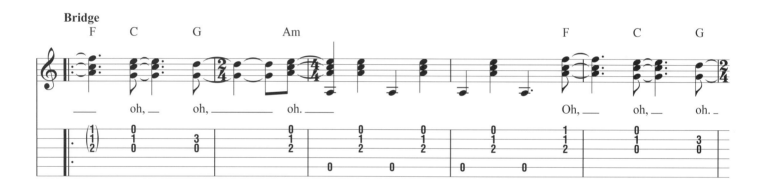

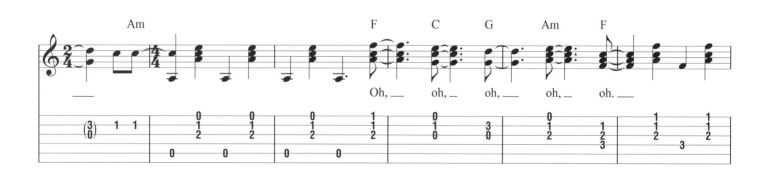

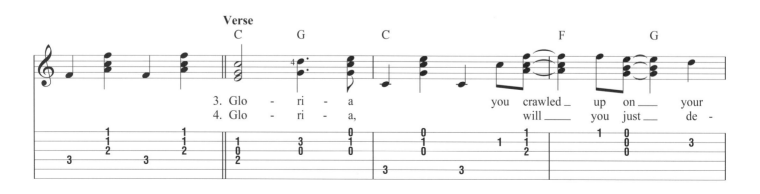

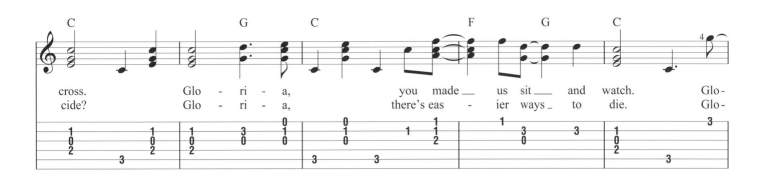

cross.   Glo - ri - a,   you made __ us sit __ and watch.   Glo-
cide?   Glo - ri - a,   there's eas - ier ways __ to die.   Glo-

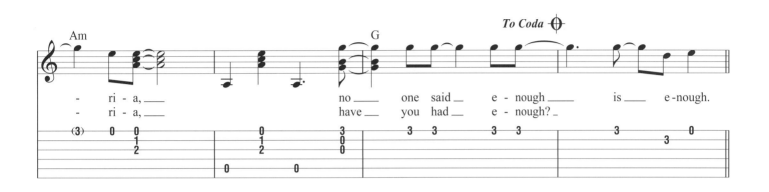

To Coda ⊕

- ri - a, ___   no __ one said __ e - nough __ is __ e-nough.
- ri - a, ___   have __ you had __ e - nough? __

Interlude

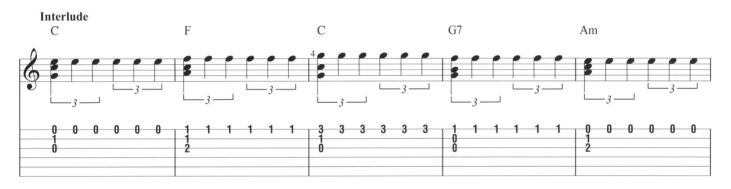

⊕ **Coda**

D.S. al Coda   **Outro**

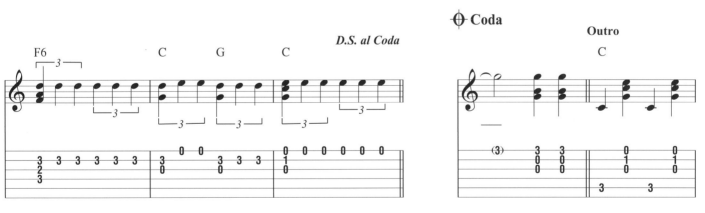

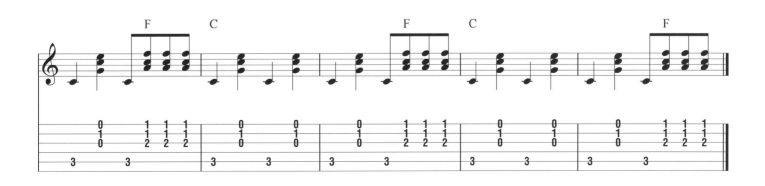

If I Can't Have You

Words and Music by Shawn Mendes, Teddy Geiger, Nate Mercereau and Scott Harris

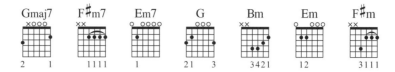

Strum Pattern: 5
Pick Pattern: 2

Chorus
Moderately fast

I can't write one song that's not a-bout you. Can't drink with-out think-ing a-bout

you. Is it too late to tell you that ev-'ry-thing means noth-ing if I can't have you?

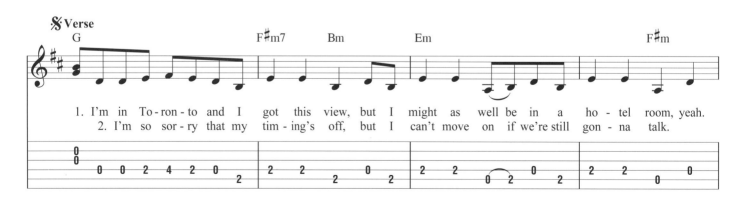

1. I'm in To-ron-to and I got this view, but I might as well be in a ho-tel room, yeah.
2. I'm so sor-ry that my tim-ing's off, but I can't move on if we're still gon-na talk.

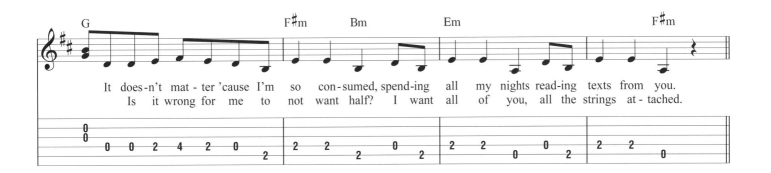

It does-n't mat - ter 'cause I'm so con-sumed, spend-ing all my nights read-ing texts from you.
Is it wrong for me to not want half? I want all of you, all the strings at - tached.

Pre-Chorus

Oh, I'm good at keep-ing my dis-tance. I know that you're the feel-ing I'm miss-ing. You _

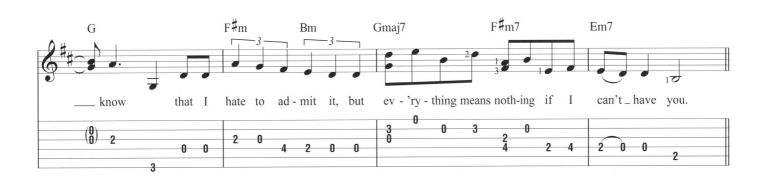

_ know that I hate to ad - mit it, but ev - 'ry - thing means noth-ing if I can't _ have you.

Chorus

I can't write one song that's _ not a-bout you. Can't drink with - out think - ing a-bout

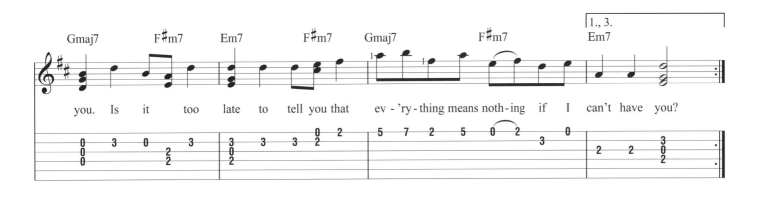

you. Is it too late to tell you that ev - 'ry-thing means noth-ing if I can't have you?

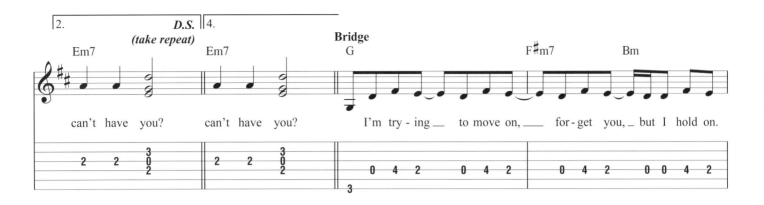

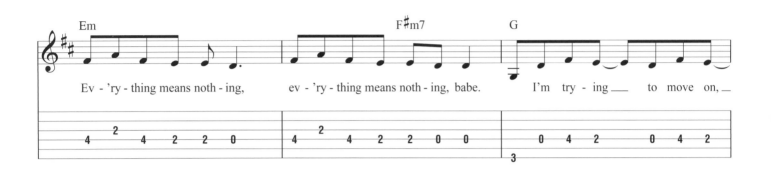

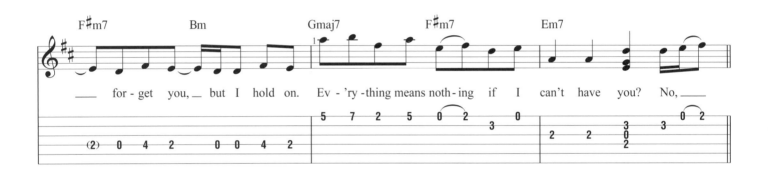

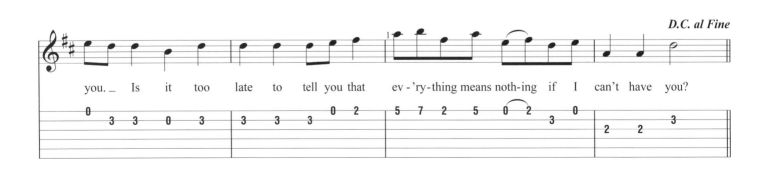

Lo/Hi

Words and Music by Dan Auerbach and Patrick Carney

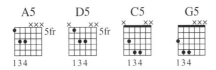

Strum Pattern: 1
Pick Pattern: 5

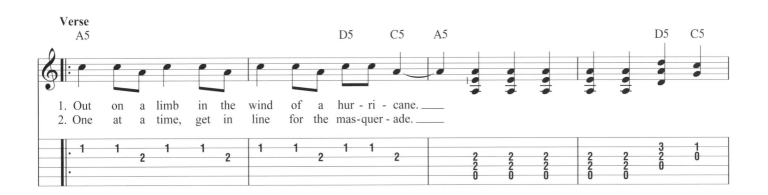

Pre-Chorus

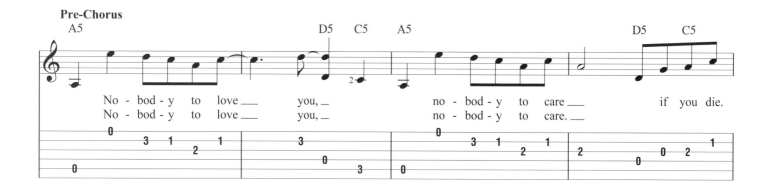

No - bod - y to love ___ you, ___ no - bod - y to care ___ if you die.
No - bod - y to love ___ you, ___ no - bod - y to care. ___

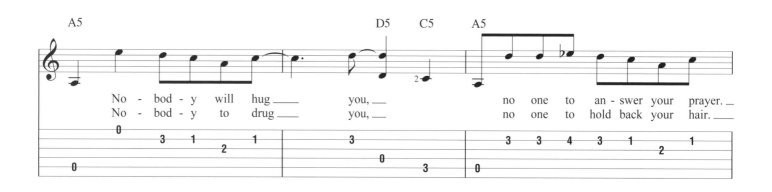

No - bod - y will hug ___ you, ___ no one to an - swer your prayer. ___
No - bod - y to drug ___ you, ___ no one to hold back your hair. ___

Chorus

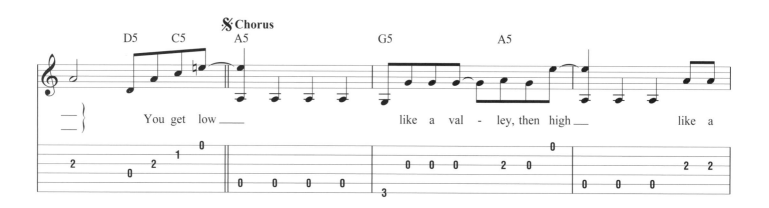

You get low ___ like a val - ley, then high ___ like a

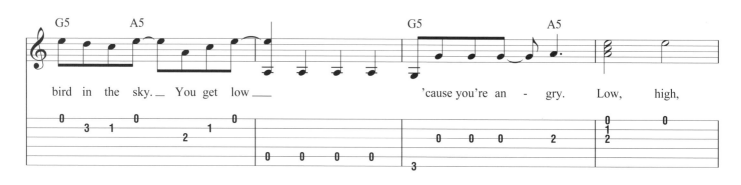

bird in the sky. ___ You get low ___ 'cause you're an - gry. Low, high,

Look What God Gave Her

Words and Music by Thomas Rhett, Ammar Malik, Jacob Hindlin, Julian Bunetta, John Ryan and Rhett Akins

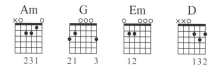

Strum Pattern: 6
Pick Pattern: 3

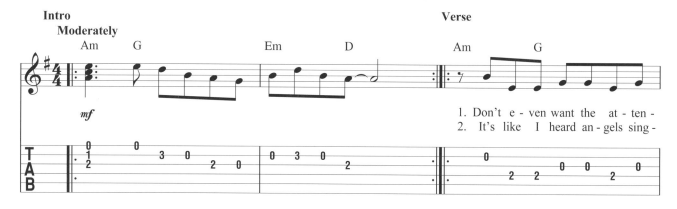

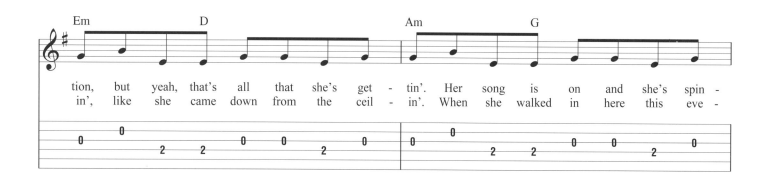

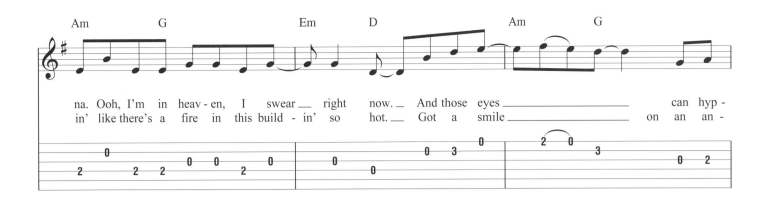

na. Ooh, I'm in heav-en, I swear ___ right now. ___ And those eyes _____ can hyp-
in' like there's a fire in this build-in' so hot. ___ Got a smile _____ on an an-

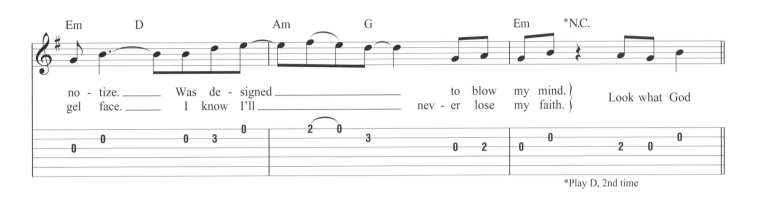

no-tize. _____ Was de-signed _____ to blow my mind. }
gel face. _____ I know I'll _____ nev-er lose my faith. } Look what God

*Play D, 2nd time

§ **Chorus**

gave her, how per-fect He made her. She walks in the room, ___ it's like He an-swered my

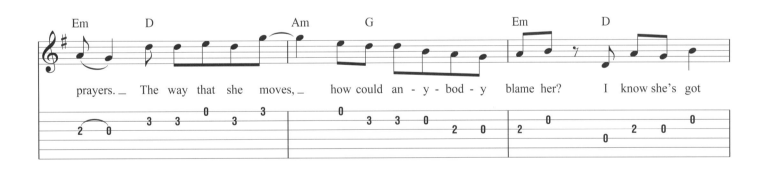

prayers. ___ The way that she moves, ___ how could an-y-bod-y blame her? I know she's got

Interlude

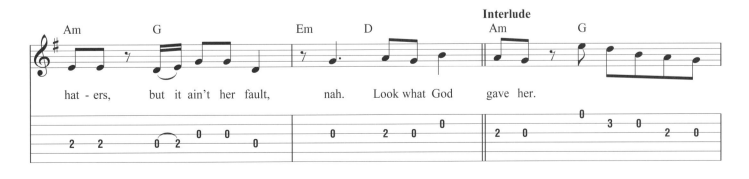

hat-ers, but it ain't her fault, nah. Look what God gave her.

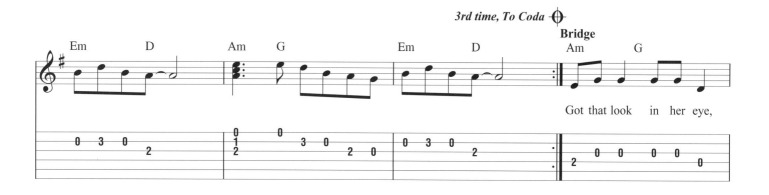

Bridge

Got that look in her eye,

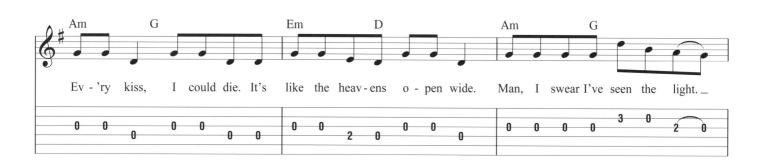

swear she fell right out the sky. Yeah, I think I've seen the light.

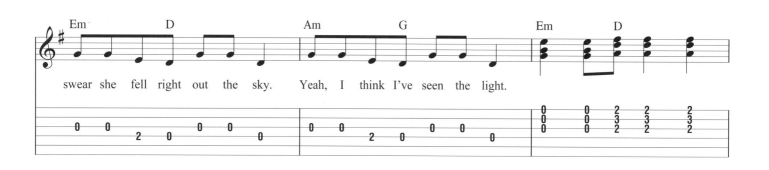

Ev-'ry kiss, I could die. It's like the heav-ens o-pen wide. Man, I swear I've seen the light.

D.S. al Coda   ⊕ **Coda**

Outro

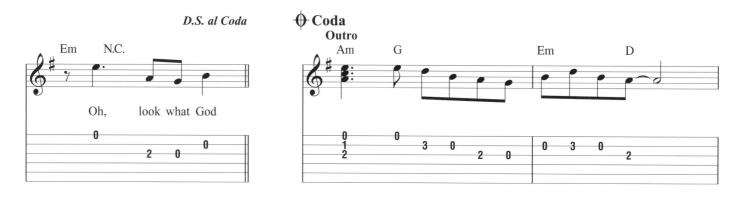

Oh, look what God

Look what God gave her.

Speechless

from ALADDIN

Music by Alan Menken
Lyrics by Benj Pasek and Justin Paul

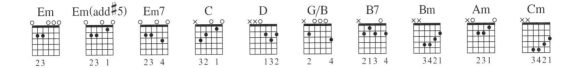

*Capo II

Strum Pattern: 3
Pick Pattern: 1

Intro
Slow, in 2

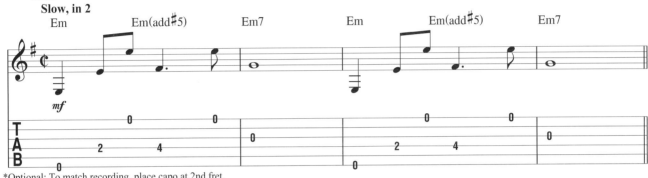

*Optional: To match recording, place capo at 2nd fret.

Verse

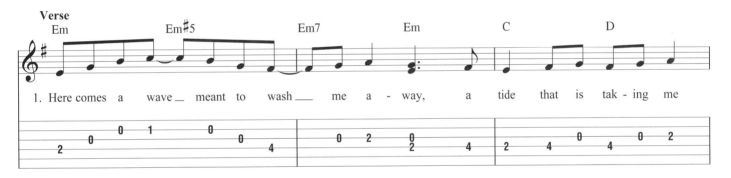

1. Here comes a wave ___ meant to wash ___ me a-way, a tide that is tak-ing me

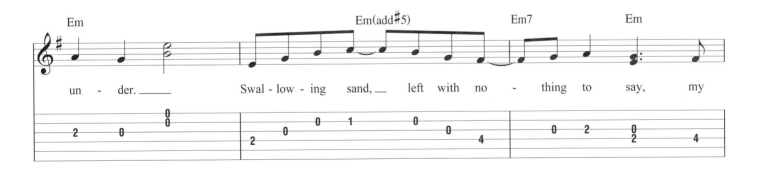

un-der. ___ Swal-low-ing sand, ___ left with no-thing to say, my

voice drowned out ___ in the thun-der. ___ But I won't

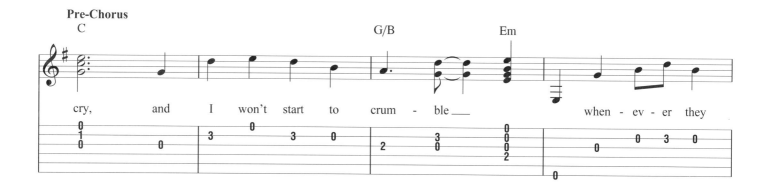

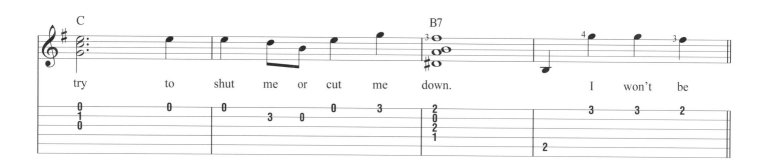

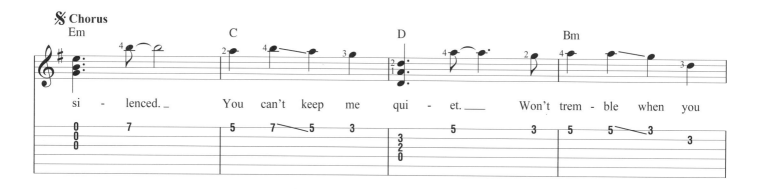

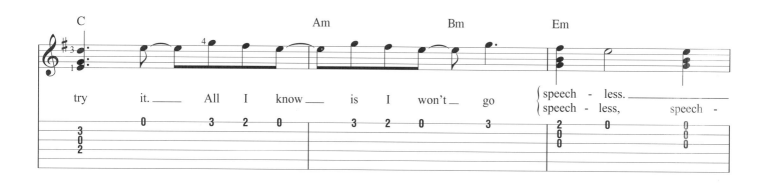

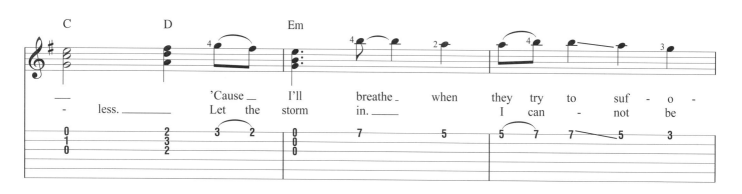

cate me. ____ Don't you un - der - es - ti - mate me, _____ }'cause I know ____
bro - ken. ____ No, I won't live un - spo - ken, _____

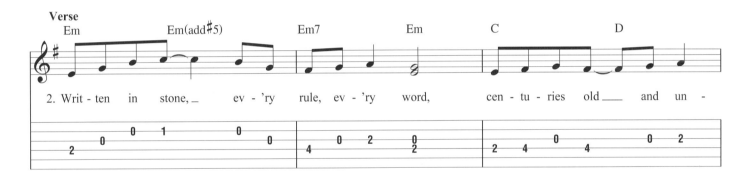

To Coda ⊕

____ that I won't __ go speech - less.

*N.C. 1st time only

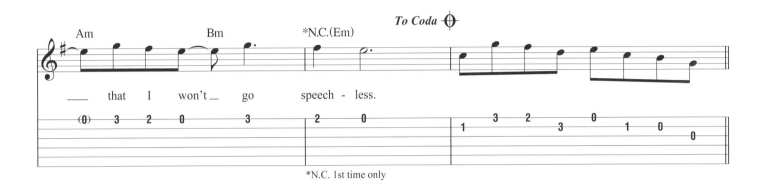

Verse

2. Writ - ten in stone, ___ ev - 'ry rule, ev - 'ry word, cen - tu - ries old ___ and un -

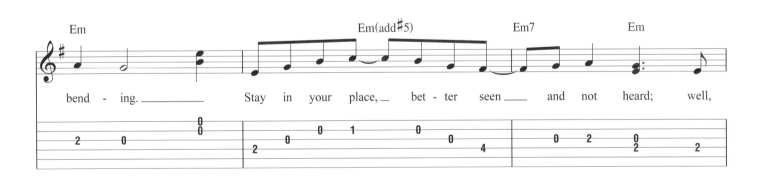

bend - ing. _____ Stay in your place, __ bet - ter seen ___ and not heard; well,

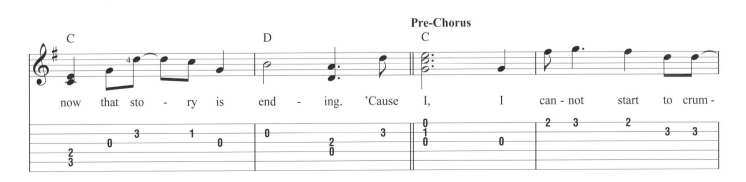

Pre-Chorus

now that sto - ry is end - ing. 'Cause I, I can - not start to crum -

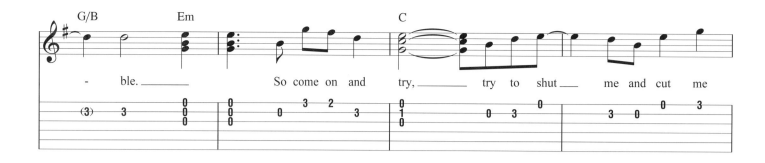

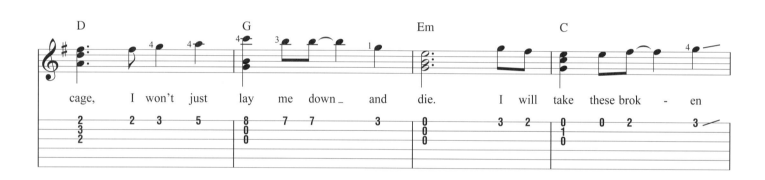

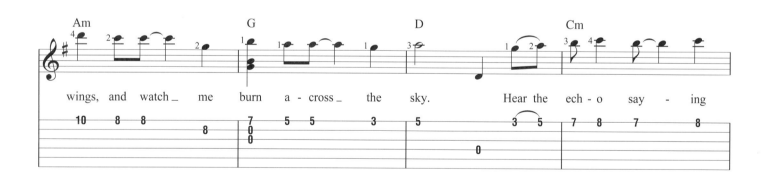

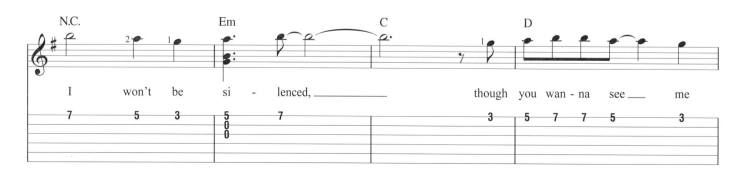

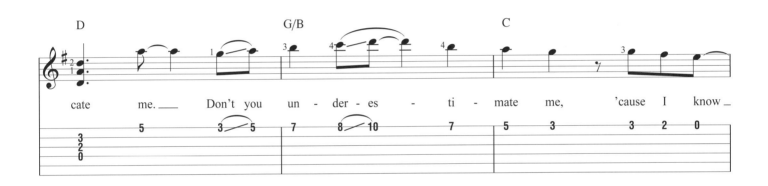

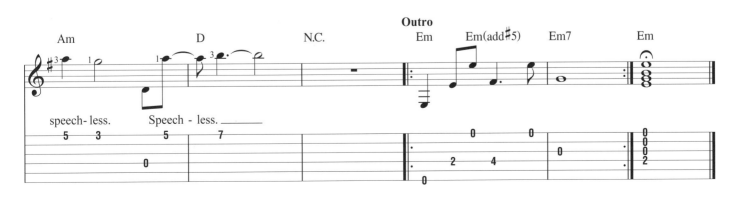

ME!

Words and Music by Taylor Swift, Joel Little and Brendon Urie

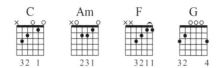

Strum Pattern: 4, 1
Pick Pattern: 3, 1

Intro
Moderately slow, in 2

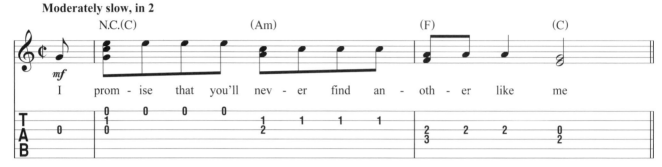

I prom-ise that you'll nev-er find an-oth-er like me

Verse

1. I know that I'm a hand-ful, ba-by, uh. I know I nev-er think be-fore I

ee. 2. *See additional lyrics*

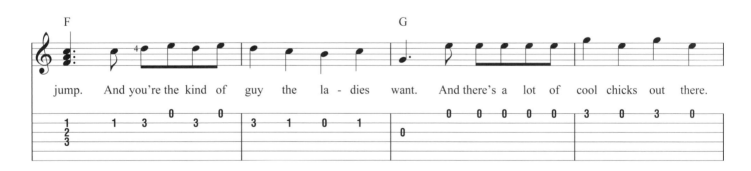

jump. And you're the kind of guy the la-dies want. And there's a lot of cool chicks out there.

I know that I went psy-cho on the phone. I nev-er leave_ well e-nough a-

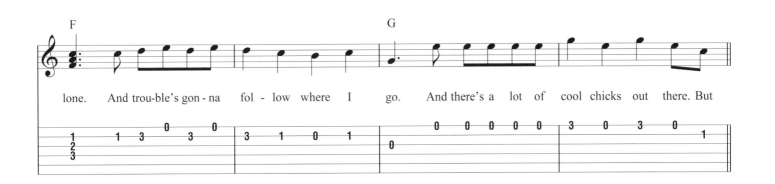

lone. And trou-ble's gon-na fol-low where I go. And there's a lot of cool chicks out there. But

Pre-Chorus

one of these things is not___ like the oth-ers.

{ Like a rain-bow with all___ of the col-lors. }
{ Liv-ing in win-ter, I___ am your sum-mer. }

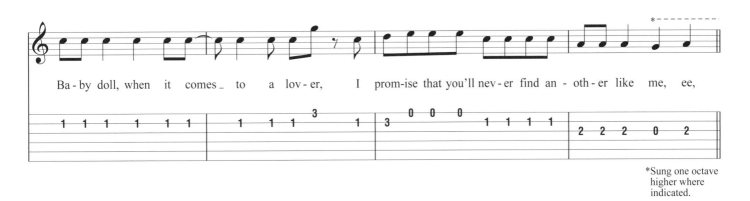

Ba-by doll, when it comes___ to a lov-er, I prom-ise that you'll nev-er find an-oth-er like me, ee,

*Sung one octave
higher where
indicated.

Chorus

C   Am   F

ee.   Oo, oo, oo.___   I'm the on-ly one of me.___

G   C

{ 1., 3. Ba-by, that's the fun of me, }
{ 2. Let me keep you com-pa-ny, } ee, ee, ee.___   Oo, oo, oo.___

Additional Lyrics

2. I know I tend to make it about me. I know you never get just what you see.
But I will never bore you, baby. And there's a lot of lame guys out there.
And when we had that fight out in the rain, you ran after me and called my name.
I never wanna see you walk away. And there's a lot of lame guys out there.
'Cause…

Señorita

Words and Music by Camila Cabello, Charlotte Aitchison, Jack Patterson, Shawn Mendes, Magnus Hoiberg, Benjamin Levin, Ali Tamposi and Andrew Wotman

Strum Pattern: 2
Pick Pattern: 4

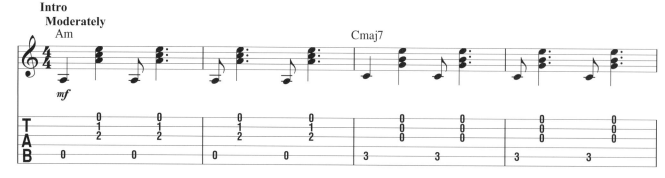

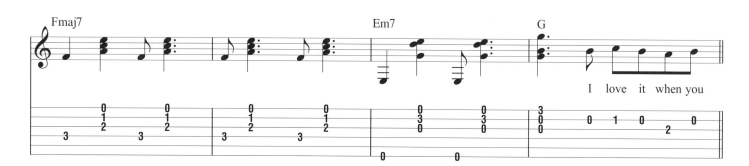

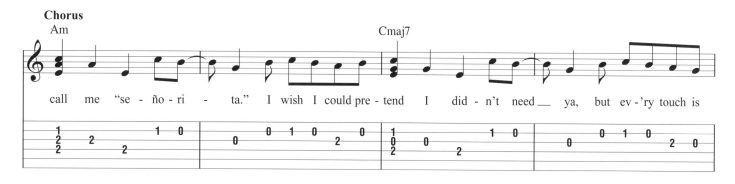

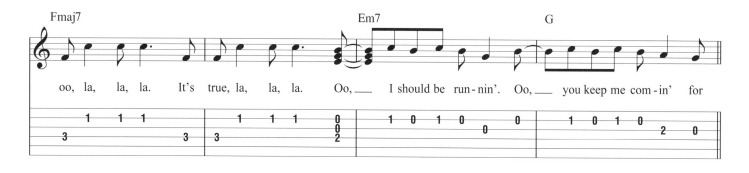

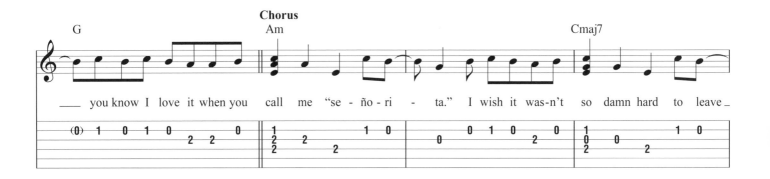

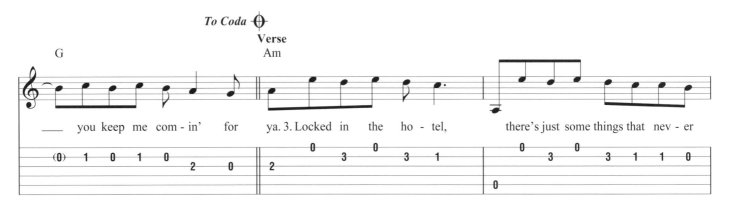

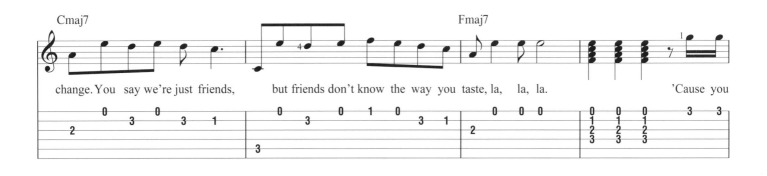

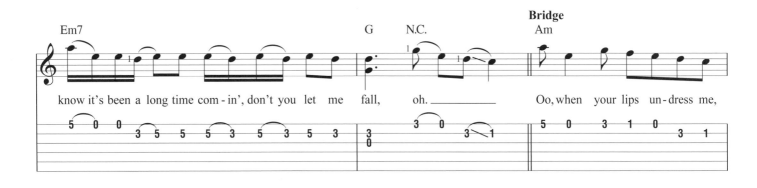

hooked on   your tongue.   Oo, love, your kiss is dead - ly. Don't stop. I love it when you

⊕ Coda
Outro

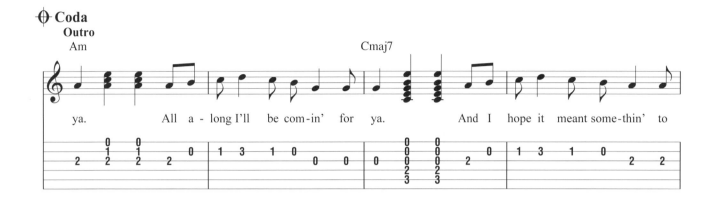

ya.   All a - long I'll be com - in' for ya.   And I hope it meant some-thin' to

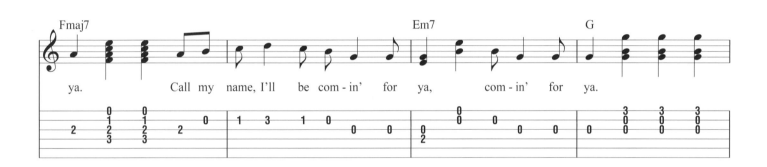

ya.   Call my name, I'll be com - in' for ya,   com - in' for ya.

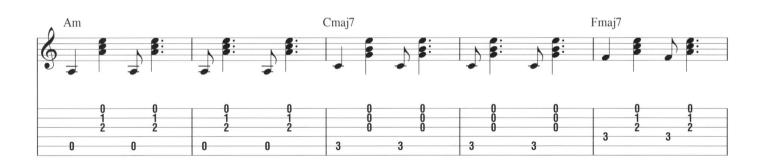

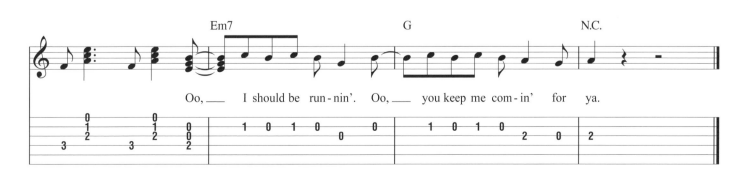

Oo, ___ I should be run - nin'. Oo, ___ you keep me com - in' for ya.

Someone You Loved

Words and Music by Lewis Capaldi, Benjamin Kohn, Peter Kelleher, Thomas Barnes and Samuel Roman

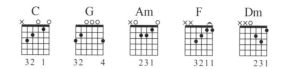

*Capo I

Strum Pattern: 1
Pick Pattern: 5

Intro
Moderately

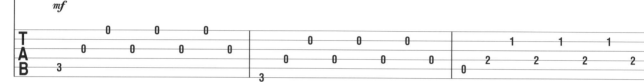

*Optional: To match recording, place capo at 1st fret.

Verse

1. I'm go-ing un-der, and this time I fear there's no one to save ___
2. I'm go-ing un-der, and this time I fear there's no one to turn ___

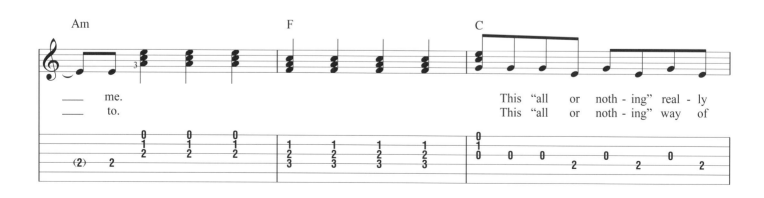

___ me.
___ to.

This "all or noth-ing" real-ly
This "all or noth-ing" way of

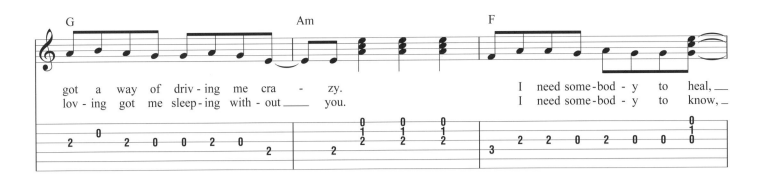

got a way of driv-ing me cra - zy.
lov - ing got me sleep-ing with-out ____ you.
I need some-bod - y to heal, ____
I need some-bod - y to know, ____

____ some-bod - y to know, ____ some-bod - y to have, ____ some-bod - y to hold.
____ some-bod - y to heal, ____ some-bod - y to have just to know how it feels.

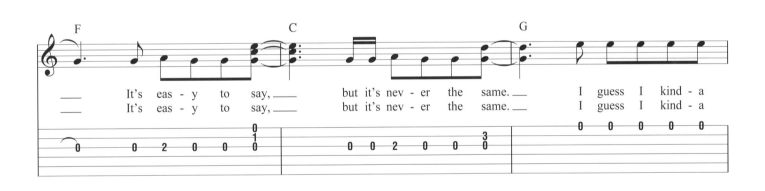

____ It's eas - y to say, ____ but it's nev - er the same. ____ I guess I kind - a
____ It's eas - y to say, ____ but it's nev - er the same. ____ I guess I kind - a

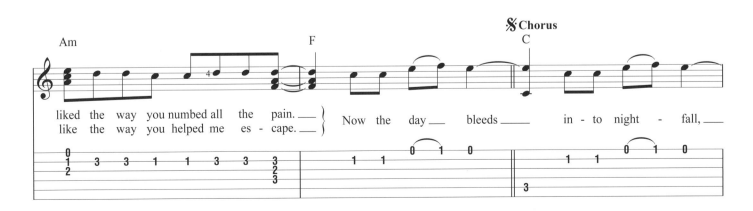

liked the way you numbed all the pain. ____
like the way you helped me es - cape. ____
Now the day ____ bleeds ____ in - to night - fall, ____

%Chorus

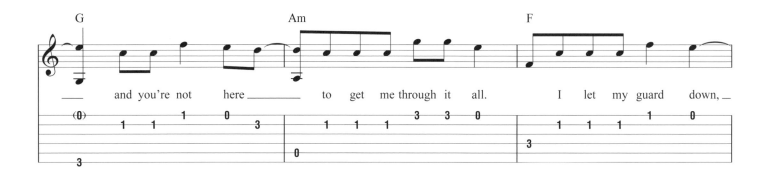

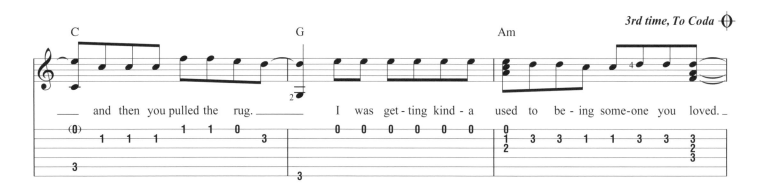

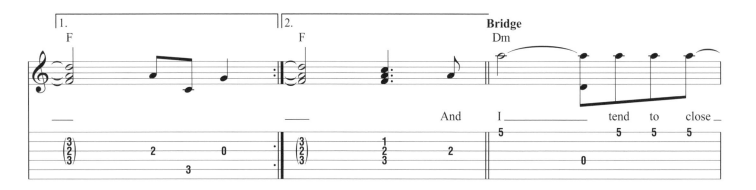

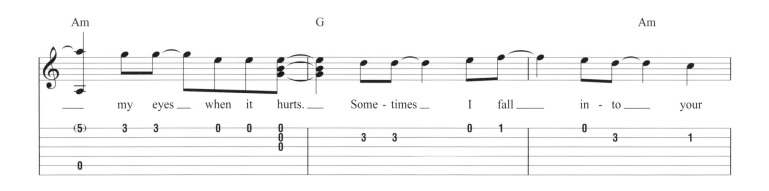

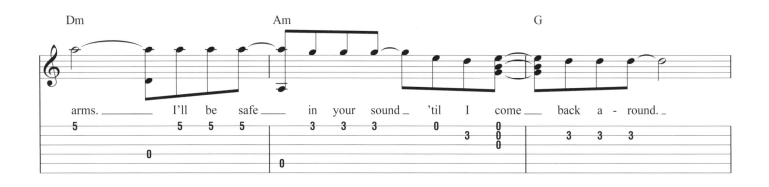

44

*Let chords ring, next 6 meas.

D.S. al Coda

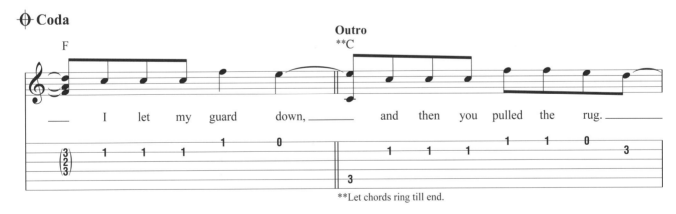

**Let chords ring till end.

Whiskey Glasses

Words and Music by Kevin Kadish and Ben Burgess

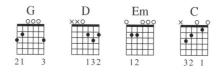

*Tune down 1/2 step:
(low to high) E♭-A♭-D♭-G♭-B♭-E♭

Strum Pattern: 3
Pick Pattern: 1

Verse
Moderately slow, in 2

mf

1. Pour _____ me. _____ pour ___ me an-oth-er drink. 'Cause

*Optional: To match recording, tune down 1/2 step.

I don't wan-na feel a thing, ___ no more, hell, naw. I just wan-na sip it till the pain wears

Verse
G

off. 2. Pour _____ me, _____ pour ___ me an-oth-er round. Line ___
3. *See additional lyrics*

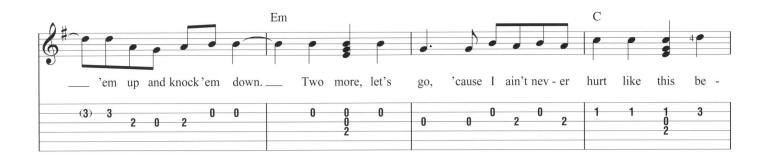

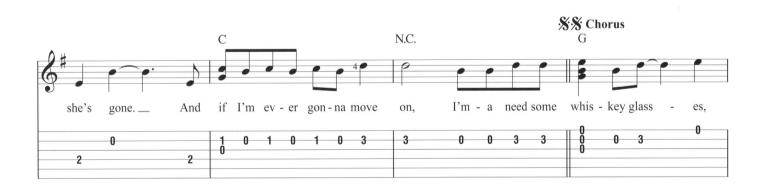

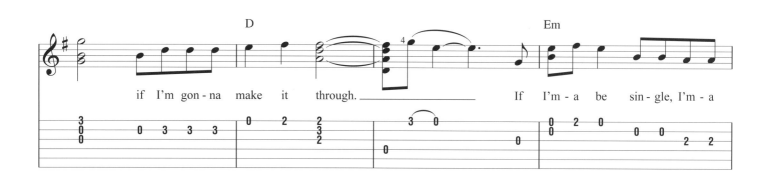

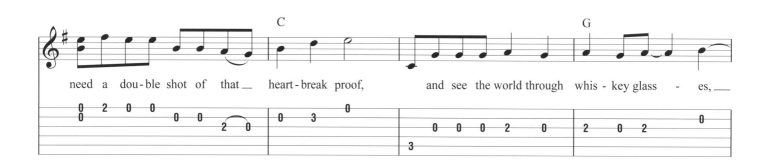

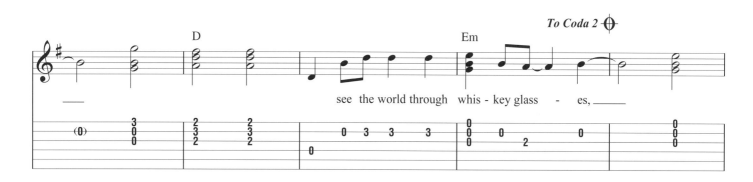

Coda 1

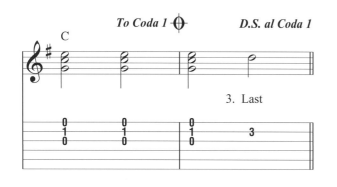

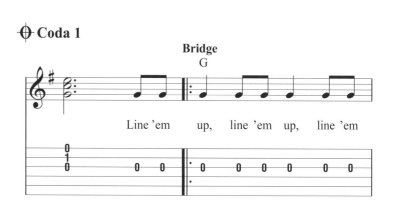

Additional Lyrics

3. Last call, I swear this'll be my last call.
   Now, I ain't drunk dialin'
   No more at three A.M.
   Mister Bartender, hit me again.

Sucker

Words and Music by Nick Jonas, Joseph Jonas, Miles Ale,
Ryan Tedder, Louis Bell, Adam Feeney and Kevin Jonas

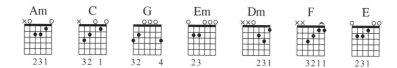

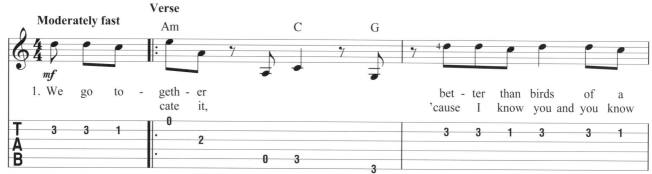

*Capo IV

Strum Pattern: 1
Pick Pattern: 1

Verse

Moderately fast

mf

1. We go to - geth - er
   cate it,   bet - ter than birds of a
                            'cause I know you and you know

*Optional: To match recording, place capo at 4th fret.

feath - er, you and me.
ev - 'ry - thing a - bout me.   We change the weath - er,   yeah. —
                                       I can't re - mem - ber,   yeah, —

I'm feel - ing heat in De - cem - ber when you're 'round me.
all of the nights I don't re - mem - ber when you're 'round me.   I've been danc -

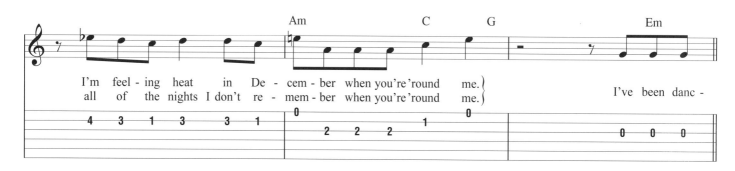

Pre-Chorus

ing on top of cars — and stum - bl - ing out of bars. — I fol - low you through the dark, — can't get

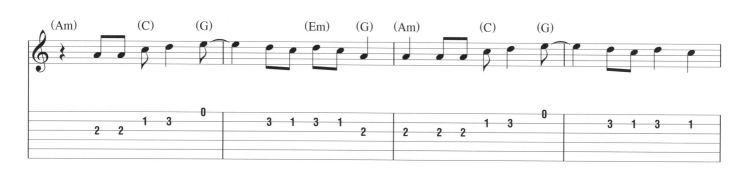

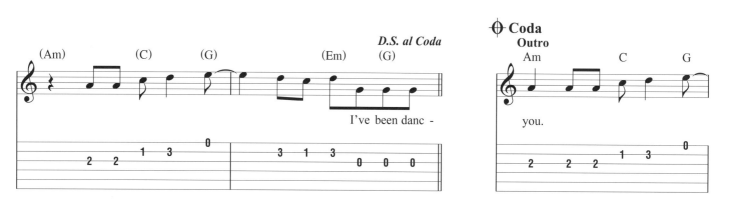

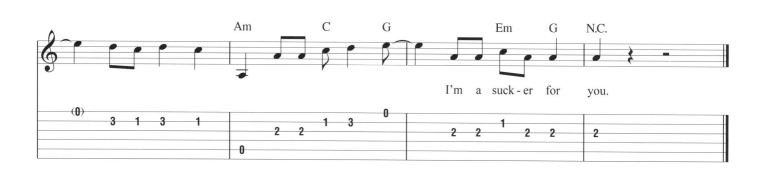

EASY GUITAR WITH NOTES & TAB

This series features simplified arrangements with notes, tab, chord charts, and strum and pick patterns.

MIXED FOLIOS

00702287	Acoustic	$16.99
00702002	Acoustic Rock Hits for Easy Guitar	$15.99
00702166	All-Time Best Guitar Collection	$19.99
00702232	Best Acoustic Songs for Easy Guitar	$14.99
00119835	Best Children's Songs	$16.99
00702233	Best Hard Rock Songs	$15.99
00703055	The Big Book of Nursery Rhymes & Children's Songs	$16.99
00322179	The Big Easy Book of Classic Rock Guitar	$24.95
00698978	Big Christmas Collection	$17.99
00702394	Bluegrass Songs for Easy Guitar	$12.99
00289632	Bohemian Rhapsody	$17.99
00703387	Celtic Classics	$14.99
00224808	Chart Hits of 2016-2017	$14.99
00267383	Chart Hits of 2017-2018	$14.99
00702149	Children's Christian Songbook	$9.99
00702028	Christmas Classics	$8.99
00101779	Christmas Guitar	$14.99
00702185	Christmas Hits	$10.99
00702141	Classic Rock	$8.95
00159642	Classical Melodies	$12.99
00253933	Disney/Pixar's Coco	$16.99
00702203	CMT's 100 Greatest Country Songs	$29.99

00702283	The Contemporary Christian Collection	$16.99
00196954	Contemporary Disney	$16.99
00702239	Country Classics for Easy Guitar	$22.99
00702257	Easy Acoustic Guitar Songs	$14.99
00702280	Easy Guitar Tab White Pages	$29.99
00702041	Favorite Hymns for Easy Guitar	$10.99
00222701	Folk Pop Songs	$14.99
00140841	4-Chord Hymns for Guitar	$9.99
00702281	4 Chord Rock	$10.99
00126894	Frozen	$14.99
00702286	Glee	$16.99
00699374	Gospel Favorites	$16.99
00702160	The Great American Country Songbook	$16.99
00702050	Great Classical Themes for Easy Guitar	$8.99
00702116	Greatest Hymns for Guitar	$10.99
00275088	The Greatest Showman	$17.99
00148030	Halloween Guitar Songs	$14.99
00702273	Irish Songs	$12.99
00192503	Jazz Classics for Easy Guitar	$14.99
00702275	Jazz Favorites for Easy Guitar	$15.99
00702274	Jazz Standards for Easy Guitar	$16.99
00702162	Jumbo Easy Guitar Songbook	$19.99
00232285	La La Land	$16.99
00702258	Legends of Rock	$14.99
00702189	MTV's 100 Greatest Pop Songs	$24.95

00702272	1950s Rock	$15.99
00702271	1960s Rock	$15.99
00702270	1970s Rock	$16.99
00702269	1980s Rock	$15.99
00702268	1990s Rock	$19.99
00109725	Once	$14.99
00702187	Selections from O Brother Where Art Thou?	$17.99
00702178	100 Songs for Kids	$14.99
00702515	Pirates of the Caribbean	$14.99
00702125	Praise and Worship for Guitar	$10.99
00287930	Songs from *A Star Is Born, The Greatest Showman, La La Land,* and More Movie Musicals	$16.99
00702285	Southern Rock Hits	$12.99
00156420	Star Wars Music	$14.99
00121535	30 Easy Celtic Guitar Solos	$15.99
00702220	Today's Country Hits	$12.99
00121900	Today's Women of Pop & Rock	$14.99
00244654	Top Hits of 2017	$14.99
00283786	Top Hits of 2018	$14.99
00702294	Top Worship Hits	$15.99
00702255	VH1's 100 Greatest Hard Rock Songs	$27.99
00702175	VH1's 100 Greatest Songs of Rock and Roll	$24.99
00702253	Wicked	$12.99

ARTIST COLLECTIONS

00702267	AC/DC for Easy Guitar	$15.99
00702598	Adele for Easy Guitar	$15.99
00156221	Adele – 25	$16.99
00702040	Best of the Allman Brothers	$16.99
00702865	J.S. Bach for Easy Guitar	$14.99
00702169	Best of The Beach Boys	$12.99
00702292	The Beatles — 1	$19.99
00125796	Best of Chuck Berry	$15.99
00702201	The Essential Black Sabbath	$12.95
02501615	Zac Brown Band — The Foundation	$16.99
02501621	Zac Brown Band — You Get What You Give	$16.99
00702043	Best of Johnny Cash	$16.99
00702090	Eric Clapton's Best	$12.99
00702086	Eric Clapton — from the Album Unplugged	$15.99
00702202	The Essential Eric Clapton	$14.99
00702250	blink-182 — Greatest Hits	$15.99
00702053	Best of Patsy Cline	$15.99
00222697	Very Best of Coldplay – 2nd Edition	$14.99
00702229	The Very Best of Creedence Clearwater Revival	$15.99
00702145	Best of Jim Croce	$15.99
00702278	Crosby, Stills & Nash	$12.99
14042809	Bob Dylan	$14.99
00702276	Fleetwood Mac — Easy Guitar Collection	$14.99
00139462	The Very Best of Grateful Dead	$15.99
00702136	Best of Merle Haggard	$14.99
00702227	Jimi Hendrix — Smash Hits	$16.99
00702288	Best of Hillsong United	$12.99
00702236	Best of Antonio Carlos Jobim	$14.99
00702245	Elton John — Greatest Hits 1970–2002	$17.99

00129855	Jack Johnson	$16.99
00702204	Robert Johnson	$10.99
00702234	Selections from Toby Keith — 35 Biggest Hits	$12.95
00702003	Kiss	$12.99
00702216	Lynyrd Skynyrd	$15.99
00702182	The Essential Bob Marley	$14.99
00146081	Maroon 5	$14.99
00121925	Bruno Mars – Unorthodox Jukebox	$12.99
00702248	Paul McCartney — All the Best	$14.99
00702129	Songs of Sarah McLachlan	$12.95
00125484	The Best of MercyMe	$12.99
02501316	Metallica — Death Magnetic	$19.99
00702209	Steve Miller Band — Young Hearts (Greatest Hits)	$12.95
00124167	Jason Mraz	$15.99
00702096	Best of Nirvana	$15.99
00702211	The Offspring — Greatest Hits	$12.95
00138026	One Direction	$14.99
00702030	Best of Roy Orbison	$15.99
00702144	Best of Ozzy Osbourne	$14.99
00702279	Tom Petty	$12.99
00102911	Pink Floyd	$16.99
00702139	Elvis Country Favorites	$16.99
00702293	The Very Best of Prince	$15.99
00699415	Best of Queen for Guitar	$15.99
00109279	Best of R.E.M.	$14.99
00702208	Red Hot Chili Peppers — Greatest Hits	$15.99
00198960	The Rolling Stones	$16.99
00174793	The Very Best of Santana	$14.99
00702196	Best of Bob Seger	$12.95
00146046	Ed Sheeran	$14.99
00702252	Frank Sinatra — Nothing But the Best	$12.99

00702010	Best of Rod Stewart	$16.99
00702049	Best of George Strait	$14.99
00702259	Taylor Swift for Easy Guitar	$15.99
00254499	Taylor Swift – Easy Guitar Anthology	$19.99
00702260	Taylor Swift — Fearless	$14.99
00139727	Taylor Swift — 1989	$17.99
00115960	Taylor Swift — Red	$16.99
00253667	Taylor Swift — Reputation	$17.99
00702290	Taylor Swift — Speak Now	$16.99
00232849	Chris Tomlin Collection – 2nd Edition	$14.99
00702226	Chris Tomlin — See the Morning	$12.95
00148643	Train	$14.99
00702427	U2 — 18 Singles	$16.99
00702108	Best of Stevie Ray Vaughan	$16.99
00279005	The Who	$14.99
00702123	Best of Hank Williams	$14.99
00194548	Best of John Williams	$14.99
00702111	Stevie Wonder — Guitar Collection	$9.95
00702228	Neil Young — Greatest Hits	$15.99
00119133	Neil Young — Harvest	$14.99

Prices, contents and availability subject to change without notice.

Visit Hal Leonard online at **halleonard.com**

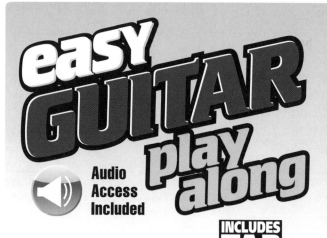

easy GUITAR play along

Audio Access Included

INCLUDES TAB

The *Easy Guitar Play Along* series features streamlined transcriptions of your favorite songs. Just follow the tab, listen to the audio to hear how the guitar should sound, and then play along using the backing tracks. Playback tools are provided for slowing down the tempo without changing pitch and looping challenging parts. The melody and lyrics are included in the book so that you can sing or simply follow along.

1. ROCK CLASSICS

Jailbreak • Living After Midnight • Mississippi Queen • Rocks Off • Runnin' Down a Dream • Smoke on the Water • Strutter • Up Around the Bend.
00702560 Book/CD Pack....... $14.99

2. ACOUSTIC TOP HITS

About a Girl • I'm Yours • The Lazy Song • The Scientist • 21 Guns • Upside Down • What I Got • Wonderwall.
00702569 Book/CD Pack....... $14.99

3. ROCK HITS

All the Small Things • Best of You • Brain Stew (The Godzilla Remix) • Californication • Island in the Sun • Plush • Smells Like Teen Spirit • Use Somebody.
00702570 Book/CD Pack....... $14.99

4. ROCK 'N' ROLL

Blue Suede Shoes • I Get Around • I'm a Believer • Jailhouse Rock • Oh, Pretty Woman • Peggy Sue • Runaway • Wake Up Little Susie.
00702572 Book/CD Pack....... $14.99

6. CHRISTMAS SONGS

Have Yourself a Merry Little Christmas • A Holly Jolly Christmas • The Little Drummer Boy • Run Rudolph Run • Santa Claus Is Comin' to Town • Silver and Gold • Sleigh Ride • Winter Wonderland.
00101879 Book/CD Pack......... $14.99

7. BLUES SONGS FOR BEGINNERS

Come On (Part 1) • Double Trouble • Gangster of Love • I'm Ready • Let Me Love You Baby • Mary Had a Little Lamb • San-Ho-Zay • T-Bone Shuffle.
00103235 Book/Online Audio $14.99

8. ACOUSTIC SONGS FOR BEGINNERS

Barely Breathing • Drive • Everlong • Good Riddance (Time of Your Life) • Hallelujah • Hey There Delilah • Lake of Fire • Photograph.
00103240 Book/CD Pack $15.99

9. ROCK SONGS FOR BEGINNERS

Are You Gonna Be My Girl • Buddy Holly • Everybody Hurts • In Bloom • Otherside • The Rock Show • Santa Monica • When I Come Around.
00103255 Book/CD Pack.....$14.99

10. GREEN DAY

Basket Case • Boulevard of Broken Dreams • Good Riddance (Time of Your Life) • Holiday • Longview • 21 Guns • Wake Me up When September Ends • When I Come Around.
00122322 Book/CD Pack $14.99

11. NIRVANA

All Apologies • Come As You Are • Heart Shaped Box • Lake of Fire • Lithium • The Man Who Sold the World • Rape Me • Smells Like Teen Spirit.
00122325 Book/Online Audio $14.99

13. AC/DC

Back in Black • Dirty Deeds Done Dirt Cheap • For Those About to Rock (We Salute You) • Hells Bells • Highway to Hell • Rock and Roll Ain't Noise Pollution • T.N.T. • You Shook Me All Night Long.
14042895 Book/Online Audio........$16.99

14. JIMI HENDRIX – SMASH HITS

All Along the Watchtower • Can You See Me • Crosstown Traffic • Fire • Foxey Lady • Hey Joe • Manic Depression • Purple Haze • Red House • Remember • Stone Free • The Wind Cries Mary.
00130591 Book/Online Audio........$24.99

HAL•LEONARD®
www.halleonard.com

HAL·LEONARD®
GUITAR PLAY-ALONG

AUDIO ACCESS INCLUDED

This series will help you play your favorite songs quickly and easily. Just follow the tab and listen to the audio to the hear how the guitar should sound, and then play along using the separate backing tracks. Audio files also include software to slow down the tempo without changing pitch. The melody and lyrics are included in the book so that you can sing or simply follow along.

INCLUDES TAB

VOL. 1 – ROCK	00699570 / $16.99
VOL. 2 – ACOUSTIC	00699569 / $16.99
VOL. 3 – HARD ROCK	00699573 / $17.99
VOL. 4 – POP/ROCK	00298615 / $16.99
VOL. 6 – '90S ROCK	00699572 / $16.99
VOL. 7 – BLUES	00699575 / $17.99
VOL. 8 – ROCK	00699585 / $16.99
VOL. 9 – EASY ACOUSTIC SONGS	00151708 / $16.99
VOL. 10 – ACOUSTIC	00699586 / $16.95
VOL. 13 – FOLK ROCK	00699581 / $16.99
VOL. 14 – BLUES ROCK	00699582 / $16.99
VOL. 15 – R&B	00699583 / $16.99
VOL. 16 – JAZZ	00699584 / $15.95
VOL. 17 – COUNTRY	00699588 / $16.99
VOL. 18 – ACOUSTIC ROCK	00699577 / $15.95
VOL. 20 – ROCKABILLY	00699580 / $16.99
VOL. 21 – SANTANA	00174525 / $17.99
VOL. 22 – CHRISTMAS	00699600 / $15.99
VOL. 23 – SURF	00699635 / $15.99
VOL. 24 – ERIC CLAPTON	00699649 / $17.99
VOL. 25 – THE BEATLES	00198265 / $17.99
VOL. 26 – ELVIS PRESLEY	00699643 / $16.99
VOL. 27 – DAVID LEE ROTH	00699645 / $16.95
VOL. 28 – GREG KOCH	00699646 / $17.99
VOL. 29 – BOB SEGER	00699647 / $16.99
VOL. 30 – KISS	00699644 / $16.99
VOL. 32 – THE OFFSPRING	00699653 / $14.95
VOL. 33 – ACOUSTIC CLASSICS	00699656 / $17.99
VOL. 34 – CLASSIC ROCK	00699658 / $17.99
VOL. 35 – HAIR METAL	00699660 / $17.99
VOL. 36 – SOUTHERN ROCK	00699661 / $17.99
VOL. 37 – ACOUSTIC UNPLUGGED	00699662 / $22.99
VOL. 38 – BLUES	00699663 / $16.95
VOL. 39 – '80S METAL	00699664 / $16.99
VOL. 40 – INCUBUS	00699668 / $17.95
VOL. 41 – ERIC CLAPTON	00699669 / $17.99
VOL. 42 – COVER BAND HITS	00211597 / $16.99
VOL. 43 – LYNYRD SKYNYRD	00699681 / $17.99
VOL. 44 – JAZZ	00699689 / $16.99
VOL. 45 – TV THEMES	00699718 / $14.95
VOL. 46 – MAINSTREAM ROCK	00699722 / $16.95
VOL. 47 – HENDRIX SMASH HITS	00699723 / $19.99
VOL. 48 – AEROSMITH CLASSICS	00699724 / $17.99
VOL. 49 – STEVIE RAY VAUGHAN	00699725 / $17.99
VOL. 50 – VAN HALEN 1978-1984	00110269 / $17.99
VOL. 51 – ALTERNATIVE '90S	00699727 / $14.99
VOL. 52 – FUNK	00699728 / $15.99
VOL. 53 – DISCO	00699729 / $14.99
VOL. 54 – HEAVY METAL	00699730 / $16.99
VOL. 55 – POP METAL	00699731 / $14.95
VOL. 56 – FOO FIGHTERS	00699749 / $17.99
VOL. 59 – CHET ATKINS	00702347 / $16.99
VOL. 62 – CHRISTMAS CAROLS	00699798 / $12.95
VOL. 63 – CREEDENCE CLEARWATER REVIVAL	00699802 / $16.99
VOL. 64 – THE ULTIMATE OZZY OSBOURNE	00699803 / $17.99
VOL. 66 – THE ROLLING STONES	00699807 / $17.99
VOL. 67 – BLACK SABBATH	00699808 / $16.99
VOL. 68 – PINK FLOYD – DARK SIDE OF THE MOON	00699809 / $16.99
VOL. 73 – BLUESY ROCK	00699829 / $16.99
VOL. 74 – SIMPLE STRUMMING SONGS	00151706 / $19.99
VOL. 75 – TOM PETTY	00699882 / $16.99

VOL. 76 – COUNTRY HITS	00699884 / $16.99
VOL. 77 – BLUEGRASS	00699910 / $15.99
VOL. 78 – NIRVANA	00700132 / $16.99
VOL. 79 – NEIL YOUNG	00700133 / $24.99
VOL. 80 – ACOUSTIC ANTHOLOGY	00700175 / $19.95
VOL. 81 – ROCK ANTHOLOGY	00700176 / $22.99
VOL. 82 – EASY SONGS	00700177 / $16.99
VOL. 84 – STEELY DAN	00700200 / $17.99
VOL. 85 – THE POLICE	00700269 / $16.99
VOL. 86 – BOSTON	00700465 / $16.99
VOL. 87 – ACOUSTIC WOMEN	00700763 / $14.99
VOL. 89 – REGGAE	00700468 / $15.99
VOL. 90 – CLASSICAL POP	00700469 / $14.99
VOL. 91 – BLUES INSTRUMENTALS	00700505 / $17.99
VOL. 92 – EARLY ROCK INSTRUMENTALS	00700506 / $15.99
VOL. 93 – ROCK INSTRUMENTALS	00700507 / $17.99
VOL. 94 – SLOW BLUES	00700508 / $16.99
VOL. 95 – BLUES CLASSICS	00700509 / $15.99
VOL. 96 – BEST COUNTRY HITS	00211615 / $16.99
VOL. 97 – CHRISTMAS CLASSICS	00236542 / $14.99
VOL. 99 – ZZ TOP	00700762 / $16.99
VOL. 100 – B.B. KING	00700466 / $16.99
VOL. 101 – SONGS FOR BEGINNERS	00701917 / $14.99
VOL. 102 – CLASSIC PUNK	00700769 / $14.99
VOL. 103 – SWITCHFOOT	00700773 / $16.99
VOL. 104 – DUANE ALLMAN	00700846 / $16.99
VOL. 105 – LATIN	00700939 / $16.99
VOL. 106 – WEEZER	00700958 / $14.99
VOL. 107 – CREAM	00701069 / $16.99
VOL. 108 – THE WHO	00701053 / $16.99
VOL. 109 – STEVE MILLER	00701054 / $19.99
VOL. 110 – SLIDE GUITAR HITS	00701055 / $16.99
VOL. 111 – JOHN MELLENCAMP	00701056 / $14.99
VOL. 112 – QUEEN	00701052 / $16.99
VOL. 113 – JIM CROCE	00701058 / $17.99
VOL. 114 – BON JOVI	00701060 / $16.99
VOL. 115 – JOHNNY CASH	00701070 / $16.99
VOL. 116 – THE VENTURES	00701124 / $16.99
VOL. 117 – BRAD PAISLEY	00701224 / $16.99
VOL. 118 – ERIC JOHNSON	00701353 / $16.99
VOL. 119 – AC/DC CLASSICS	00701356 / $17.99
VOL. 120 – PROGRESSIVE ROCK	00701457 / $14.99
VOL. 121 – U2	00701508 / $16.99
VOL. 122 – CROSBY, STILLS & NASH	00701610 / $16.99
VOL. 123 – LENNON & MCCARTNEY ACOUSTIC	00701614 / $16.99
VOL. 125 – JEFF BECK	00701687 / $16.99
VOL. 126 – BOB MARLEY	00701701 / $16.99
VOL. 127 – 1970S ROCK	00701739 / $16.99
VOL. 128 – 1960S ROCK	00701740 / $14.99
VOL. 129 – MEGADETH	00701741 / $17.99
VOL. 130 – IRON MAIDEN	00701742 / $17.99
VOL. 131 – 1990S ROCK	00701743 / $14.99
VOL. 132 – COUNTRY ROCK	00701757 / $15.99
VOL. 133 – TAYLOR SWIFT	00701894 / $16.99
VOL. 134 – AVENGED SEVENFOLD	00701906 / $16.99
VOL. 135 – MINOR BLUES	00151350 / $17.99
VOL. 136 – GUITAR THEMES	00701922 / $14.99
VOL. 137 – IRISH TUNES	00701966 / $15.99
VOL. 138 – BLUEGRASS CLASSICS	00701967 / $16.99
VOL. 139 – GARY MOORE	00702370 / $16.99
VOL. 140 – MORE STEVIE RAY VAUGHAN	00702396 / $17.99
VOL. 141 – ACOUSTIC HITS	00702401 / $16.99
VOL. 142 – GEORGE HARRISON	00237697 / $17.99

VOL. 143 – SLASH	00702425 / $19.99
VOL. 144 – DJANGO REINHARDT	00702531 / $16.99
VOL. 145 – DEF LEPPARD	00702532 / $17.99
VOL. 146 – ROBERT JOHNSON	00702533 / $16.99
VOL. 147 – SIMON & GARFUNKEL	14041591 / $16.99
VOL. 148 – BOB DYLAN	14041592 / $16.99
VOL. 149 – AC/DC HITS	14041593 / $17.99
VOL. 150 – ZAKK WYLDE	02501717 / $16.99
VOL. 151 – J.S. BACH	02501730 / $16.99
VOL. 152 – JOE BONAMASSA	02501751 / $19.99
VOL. 153 – RED HOT CHILI PEPPERS	00702990 / $19.99
VOL. 155 – ERIC CLAPTON – FROM THE ALBUM UNPLUGGED	00703085 / $16.99
VOL. 156 – SLAYER	00703770 / $17.99
VOL. 157 – FLEETWOOD MAC	00101382 / $16.99
VOL. 159 – WES MONTGOMERY	00102593 / $19.99
VOL. 160 – T-BONE WALKER	00102641 / $17.99
VOL. 161 – THE EAGLES – ACOUSTIC	00102659 / $17.99
VOL. 162 – THE EAGLES HITS	00102667 / $17.99
VOL. 163 – PANTERA	00103036 / $17.99
VOL. 164 – VAN HALEN 1986-1995	00110270 / $17.99
VOL. 165 – GREEN DAY	00210343 / $17.99
VOL. 166 – MODERN BLUES	00700764 / $16.99
VOL. 167 – DREAM THEATER	00111938 / $24.99
VOL. 168 – KISS	00113421 / $17.99
VOL. 169 – TAYLOR SWIFT	00115982 / $16.99
VOL. 170 – THREE DAYS GRACE	00117337 / $16.99
VOL. 171 – JAMES BROWN	00117420 / $16.99
VOL. 172 – THE DOOBIE BROTHERS	00119670 / $16.99
VOL. 173 – TRANS-SIBERIAN ORCHESTRA	00119907 / $19.99
VOL. 174 – SCORPIONS	00122119 / $16.99
VOL. 175 – MICHAEL SCHENKER	00122127 / $17.99
VOL. 176 – BLUES BREAKERS WITH JOHN MAYALL & ERIC CLAPTON	00122132 / $19.99
VOL. 177 – ALBERT KING	00123271 / $16.99
VOL. 178 – JASON MRAZ	00124165 / $17.99
VOL. 179 – RAMONES	00127073 / $16.99
VOL. 180 – BRUNO MARS	00129706 / $16.99
VOL. 181 – JACK JOHNSON	00129854 / $16.99
VOL. 182 – SOUNDGARDEN	00138161 / $17.99
VOL. 183 – BUDDY GUY	00138240 / $17.99
VOL. 184 – KENNY WAYNE SHEPHERD	00138258 / $17.99
VOL. 185 – JOE SATRIANI	00139457 / $17.99
VOL. 186 – GRATEFUL DEAD	00139459 / $17.99
VOL. 187 – JOHN DENVER	00140839 / $17.99
VOL. 188 – MÖTLEY CRUE	00141145 / $17.99
VOL. 189 – JOHN MAYER	00144350 / $17.99
VOL. 190 – DEEP PURPLE	00146152 / $17.99
VOL. 191 – PINK FLOYD CLASSICS	00146164 / $17.99
VOL. 192 – JUDAS PRIEST	00151352 / $17.99
VOL. 193 – STEVE VAI	00156028 / $19.99
VOL. 195 – METALLICA: 1983-1988	00234291 / $19.99
VOL. 196 – METALLICA: 1991-2016	00234292 / $19.99

Prices, contents, and availability subject to change without notice.

Complete song lists available online.

HAL·LEONARD®
www.halleonard.com

GUITAR *signature licks*

Signature Licks book/audio packs provide a step-by-step breakdown of "right from the record" riffs, licks, and solos so you can jam along with your favorite bands. They contain performance notes and an overview of each artist's or group's style, with note-for-note transcriptions in notes and tab. The CDs or online audio tracks feature full-band demos at both normal and slow speeds.

AC/DC
14041352.....................$22.99

AEROSMITH 1973-1979
00695106........................$22.95

AEROSMITH 1979-1998
00695219........................$22.95

DUANE ALLMAN
00696042........................$22.99

BEST OF CHET ATKINS
00695752.......................$24.99

AVENGED SEVENFOLD
00696473........................$22.99

BEST OF THE BEATLES FOR ACOUSTIC GUITAR
00695453........................$22.99

THE BEATLES BASS
00695283........................$22.99

THE BEATLES HITS
00695049.......................$24.95

JEFF BECK
00696427........................$22.99

BEST OF GEORGE BENSON
00695418........................$22.99

BEST OF BLACK SABBATH
00695249........................$22.95

BLUES BREAKERS WITH JOHN MAYALL & ERIC CLAPTON
00696374........................$22.99

BON JOVI
00696380........................$22.99

ROY BUCHANAN
00696654........................$22.99

KENNY BURRELL
00695830.......................$24.99

BEST OF CHARLIE CHRISTIAN
00695584.......................$24.99

BEST OF ERIC CLAPTON
00695038.......................$24.99

ERIC CLAPTON – FROM THE ALBUM UNPLUGGED
00695250.......................$24.95

BEST OF CREAM
00695251........................$22.95

CREEDANCE CLEARWATER REVIVAL
00695924........................$22.95

DEEP PURPLE – GREATEST HITS
00695625........................$22.99

DREAM THEATER
00111943.......................$24.99

TOMMY EMMANUEL
00696409........................$22.99

ESSENTIAL JAZZ GUITAR
00695875........................$19.99

FAMOUS ROCK GUITAR SOLOS
00695590........................$19.95

FLEETWOOD MAC
00696416........................$22.99

BEST OF FOO FIGHTERS
00695481........................$24.95

ROBBEN FORD
00695903........................$22.95

BEST OF GRANT GREEN
00695747........................$22.99

PETER GREEN
00145386........................$22.99

THE GUITARS OF ELVIS – 2ND ED.
00174800........................$22.99

BEST OF GUNS N' ROSES
00695183........................$24.99

THE BEST OF BUDDY GUY
00695186........................$22.99

JIM HALL
00695848........................$24.99

JIMI HENDRIX
00696560........................$24.99

JIMI HENDRIX – VOLUME 2
00695835........................$24.99

JOHN LEE HOOKER
00695894........................$22.99

BEST OF JAZZ GUITAR
00695586.......................$24.99

ERIC JOHNSON
00699317.......................$24.99

ROBERT JOHNSON
00695264........................$22.95

BARNEY KESSEL
00696009.......................$24.99

THE ESSENTIAL ALBERT KING
00695713........................$22.95

B.B. KING – BLUES LEGEND
00696039........................$22.99

B.B. KING – THE DEFINITIVE COLLECTION
00695635........................$22.95

B.B. KING – MASTER BLUESMAN
00699923.......................$24.99

MARK KNOPFLER
00695178.......................$24.99

LYNYRD SKYNYRD
00695872.......................$24.99

THE BEST OF YNGWIE MALMSTEEN
00695669.......................$24.99

BEST OF PAT MARTINO
00695632.......................$24.99

MEGADETH
00696421........................$22.99

WES MONTGOMERY
00695387........................$24.99

BEST OF NIRVANA
00695483........................$24.95

VERY BEST OF OZZY OSBOURNE
00695431........................$22.99

BRAD PAISLEY
00696379........................$22.99

BEST OF JOE PASS
00695730........................$22.99

JACO PASTORIUS
00695544........................$24.95

TOM PETTY
00696021........................$22.99

PINK FLOYD
00103659........................$24.99

BEST OF QUEEN
00695097........................$24.99

RADIOHEAD
00109304........................$24.99

BEST OF RAGE AGAINST THE MACHINE
00695480........................$24.95

RED HOT CHILI PEPPERS
00695173........................$22.95

RED HOT CHILI PEPPERS – GREATEST HITS
00695828........................$24.99

JERRY REED
00118236........................$22.99

BEST OF DJANGO REINHARDT
00695660.......................$24.99

BEST OF ROCK 'N' ROLL GUITAR
00695559........................$22.99

BEST OF ROCKABILLY GUITAR
00695785........................$19.99

BEST OF CARLOS SANTANA
00174664........................$22.99

BEST OF JOE SATRIANI
00695216........................$22.95

SLASH
00696576........................$22.99

SLAYER
00121281........................$22.99

THE BEST OF SOUL GUITAR
00695703........................$19.95

BEST OF SOUTHERN ROCK
00695560........................$19.95

STEELY DAN
00696015........................$22.99

MIKE STERN
00695800.......................$24.99

BEST OF SURF GUITAR
00695822........................$19.99

STEVE VAI
00673247.......................$24.99

STEVE VAI – ALIEN LOVE SECRETS: THE NAKED VAMPS
00695223........................$22.95

STEVE VAI – FIRE GARDEN: THE NAKED VAMPS
00695166........................$22.95

STEVE VAI – THE ULTRA ZONE: NAKED VAMPS
00695684........................$22.95

VAN HALEN
00110227.......................$24.99

STEVIE RAY VAUGHAN – 2ND ED.
00699316.......................$24.95

THE GUITAR STYLE OF STEVIE RAY VAUGHAN
00695155.......................$24.95

BEST OF THE VENTURES
00695772........................$19.95

THE WHO – 2ND ED.
00695561........................$22.95

JOHNNY WINTER
00695951........................$22.99

YES
00113120........................$22.99

NEIL YOUNG – GREATEST HITS
00695988........................$22.99

BEST OF ZZ TOP
00695738.......................$24.99

HAL•LEONARD®

www.halleonard.com

COMPLETE DESCRIPTIONS AND SONGLISTS ONLINE!
Prices, contents and availability subject to change without notice.

0719

305